#3 in the Molly Learns Series

Molly Learns 10 Facts About Mary Todd Lincoln

By
Marla Harms Judge
and Molly the History Dog

I pose with a living history interpreter portraying Mary Todd Lincoln.

For Bob – Thank you for all your love and support.

Copyright © 2023 Marla Harms Judge.
All rights reserved.

Book design by Madeline Littleton and
Maria Loysa-Bel Nueve-de los Angeles

ISBN Paperback 978-1-958533-39-0
ISBN Hardcover 978-1-958533-40-6

Library of Congress Control Number: 2023910361

Please write to us at: Mollythehistorydog@gmail.com
Visit: mollythehistorydog.com

Crippled Beagle Publishing, Knoxville, TN, USA
crippledbeaglepublishing.com

TODAY
is the day to learn something
NEW

Our local volunteer fire fighter, Doug, let me visit the fire station. I am sitting on a fire truck!

Hi! My name is Molly. I am a dalmatian dog. I am white with black spots. Did you know that every dalmatian's spots are different? Kind of like everyone's freckles are different!

Many people wonder why dalmatians are considered to be "fire dogs."

When firefighters used horses to pull their water pumps, the dalmatian was the perfect choice to run alongside the fire engines. They were not afraid of fire, and they got along well with the horses. The dogs acted like living sirens, barking ahead of the firemen so people would get out of the way. They stayed with the horses to help keep them calm in frightening situations.

I pose with a doll like Mrs. Lincoln might have played with as a little girl.

Mary Todd Lincoln

My human family and I like to travel and learn about famous people and places.
I have lots of fun!

Today I want to tell you 10 facts I learned about a famous American.
She was the wife of the 16th president.
Her husband was very tall.
He was 6 feet and 4 inches tall.
She was rather short.
She was only 5 feet and 2 inches tall!

Have you guessed who you are going to be learning about?
Did you guess Mary Todd Lincoln?

If you did, you are right!
Let's learn about Mary Todd Lincoln!

I had fun learning about Mrs. Lincoln.
Before her name was Mary Todd Lincoln,
her name was Mary Ann Todd.
She was born in Lexington, Kentucky.
I have been there. Have you?
Lexington is a pretty place to visit.
She was born on December 13, 1818.

December 1818

SUN	MON	TUE	WED	THU	FRI	SAT
		1	2	3	4	5
6	7	8	9	10	11	12
🎂	14	15	16	17	18	19
20	21	22	23	24	25	26
27	28	29	30	31		

This is the house where Mary Todd grew up.

Mary's family was HUGE!
Her parents had 7 children.
Sadly, Mary's mother died
while the children were small.
Her father got remarried, and he
and his new wife had 9 more children.
So, Mary had fifteen brothers and sisters.
Wow! That is a lot of kids! How many
brothers and sisters do you have?

Mary's parents had to think up many
names for all of their children.
I think I might have run out of ideas
if I had that many puppies to name!!

Mary's parents were Robert and Eliza Todd.
Their children:
Elizabeth
Frances
Levi
Mary
Robert
Ann
George

Robert Todd's second wife was Betsey Humphreys.
Their children:
Robert
Margaret
Samuel
David
Martha
Emilie
Alexander
Elodie
Katherine

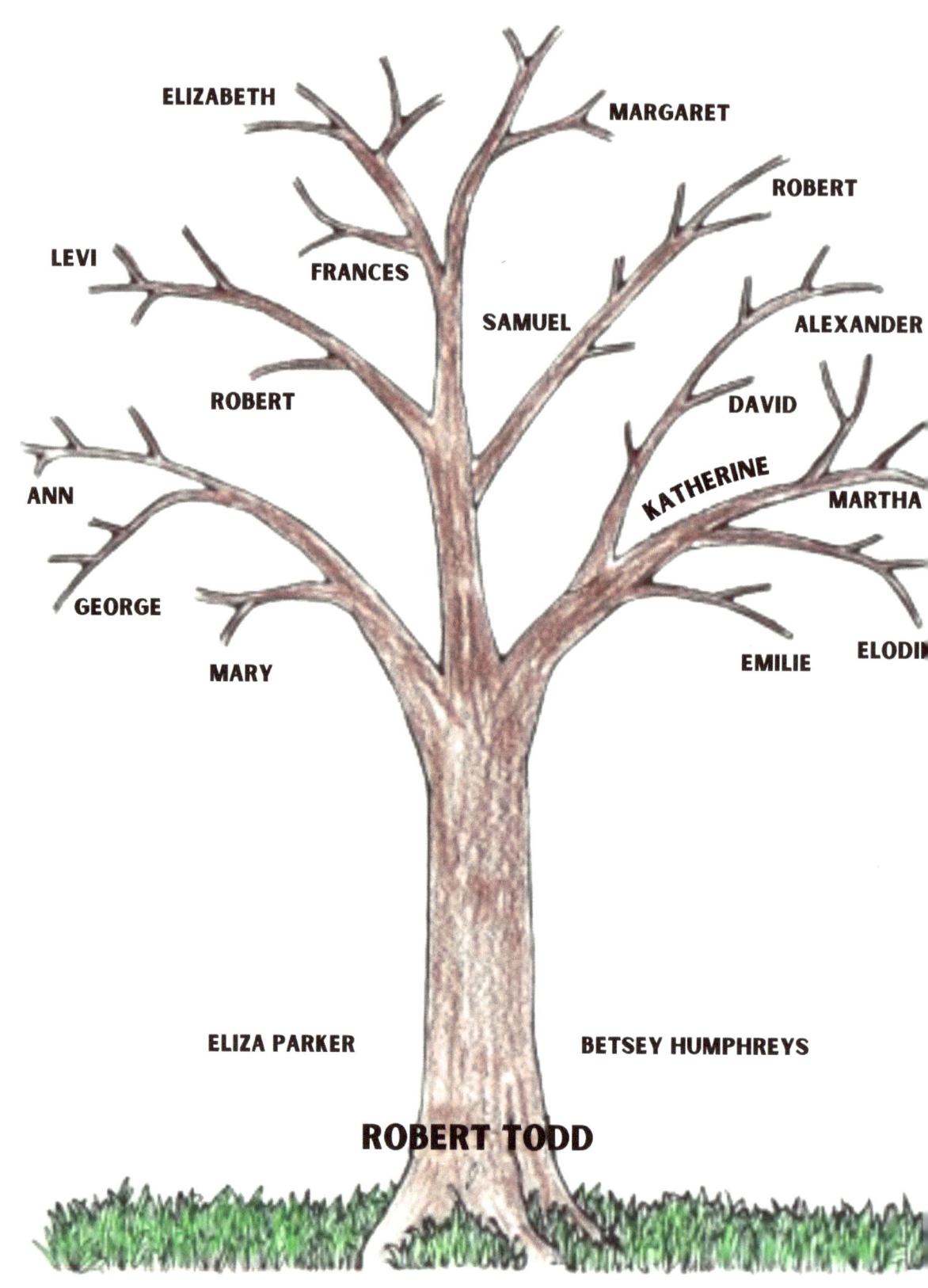

I learned many stories about Mary when she was young. When Mary was growing up, young girls were expected to act like ladies and follow the rules! She was supposed learn things that would help her take care of a house when she became a wife and mother. Girls learned things like how to knit, sew, and crochet.
Mary did not like to knit, but
she enjoyed crocheting.
Do you know how to knit or crochet?

My friend tried to teach me to knit, but it didn't work!

I also enjoyed learning about the toys Mary and all of the other children played with. They are different than toys you have today. Many of the toys and games were created to teach the children skills.

One of the games they played was rolling a big hoop with a small stick. It is much harder to do than you would think. I had fun running alongside these children who tried.

Young girls play with rolling hoops.

Another game they played was called Graces.
The game was played by 2 players.
Either 2 girls or a girl and a boy played together.
Boys did not play Graces with another boy
because it was considered a "girl's game."
Each player had 2 sticks. Using the sticks,
the players tossed and caught the hoop.
The game was meant to encourage
children to move gracefully.

Young living history interpreters show how to play Graces.

If you are not careful, your hoop may
end up in a tree! Do you think you
might like to give Graces a try?

Girls always had dolls. Parents encouraged their daughters to play with dolls so they could practice being good mothers. Girls also practiced their sewing skills by making doll clothes.

My friend is holding a doll similar to a doll Mary may have played with.

Going to school and getting an education
is important. I think it is wonderful that all
children can go to school!
I went to puppy school when I was a young pup.
(Playing fetch was my favorite part!)
I was shocked to learn that when Mary was
a young girl most people did not believe
that girls should go to school.
Luckily for Mary, her father believed in
an education for ALL of his children—
his daughters and his sons.

I always like to hear a good story.

Mary attended school for about twelve years. She studied reading, writing, grammar, arithmetic, history, geography, natural science, French, and religion. For many years Mary attended a boarding school. She lived at school during the week and went home on the weekends, like what many college students do today. They live at school but go home for visits.

Before Mary was married, she was a teacher for a short time. How amazing! Teachers are such important people in our lives, and Mary Todd Lincoln was one.

When Mary was a young woman, she traveled from her home in Lexington, Kentucky, to Springfield, Illinois, to visit her sister, Elizabeth.

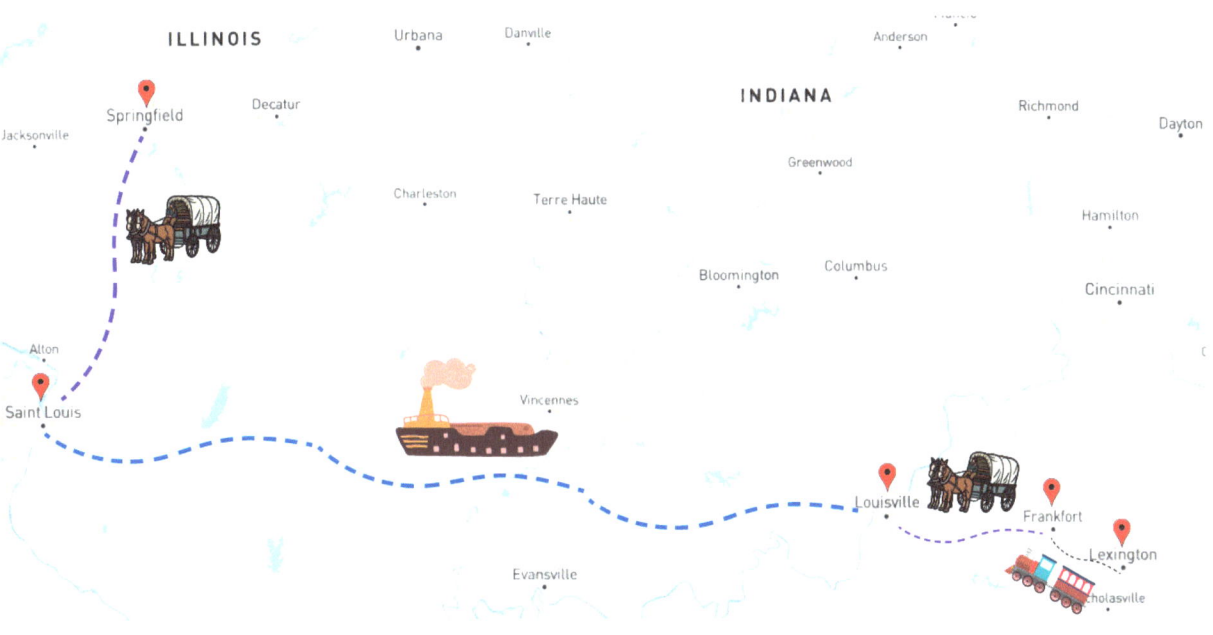

Mary had to travel by train, steamboat and stagecoach to finally arrive in Springfield. It was a long hard journey. The seats were uncomfortable. Roads were dirty, dusty, and dangerous. Today the trip would not be anything like what Mary had to endure. I like to listen to music and take a nap in the air-conditioned car when we travel! Have you ever gone on a trip with your family?

These pictures show us vehicles similar to what Mary would have traveled in to get to Springfield. They do not look very comfortable.

Mary thought it was worth the trip.
She greatly enjoyed attending parties
while she stayed with Elizabeth.
At one party she met a young man
named Abraham Lincoln.
The first time they met, Abraham said
to Mary, "Miss Todd, I would like
to dance with you in the worst way!"

Mary later told her friends, "And he did!
He danced in the *worst* way!"

I guess Mr. Lincoln's poor dancing skills
did not keep them from becoming friends,
because they eventually became
Mr. and Mrs. Abraham Lincoln!

This picture, taken at the Abraham Lincoln
Presidential Museum, shows the Lincolns
"courting" before their wedding.

The Lincolns with 3 of their sons

The Lincolns had 4 sons:
Robert, Edward, William and Thomas.
Mr. Lincoln believed that "boys will be boys."
Their sons were allowed to be mischievous!
They usually did not get into trouble
for their misbehavior!

One time, when Mary was giving
the boys a bath Willie jumped out of the tub.
He went running down the street with
no clothes on! OH MY! I think
that would have been funny to see.
Mr. Lincoln had to go catch him!

I pose with living history interpreters
portraying the Lincolns.

Young living history interpreters pose as the Lincoln boys at Lincoln Home National Historic Site.

While visiting the Lincoln Home National Historic Site, we took my picture in front of the house.

Living history interpreters portray Willie, Tad and Mrs. Lincoln's hired girl. The hired girl helped with cooking, cleaning, and looking after the boys.

Living history interpreters portray Mrs. Lincoln and 2 of her neighbors in the backyard of the Lincoln home.

I think it would have been fun to live
in the Lincolns' neighborhood.
Mrs. Lincoln loved to have parties.
There was always a lot of delicious food.
Mary liked to have what she called
"berry parties."

She would serve strawberries
and cream to her guests.
The adults would sit and visit
while the children played.
Sounds like fun to me!

Living history interpreters portraying Mary
and Abraham greet guests in their entrance way.

One yummy thing I learned about
Mrs. Lincoln is that she was a good cook.
One of President Lincoln's favorite things
for her to make was her neighborhood-famous
WHITE ALMOND CAKE.
It certainly looks delicious.
I wish I could eat some!

Would you like to try to bake
Mrs. Lincoln's cake?
I found the recipe for you!
Here are the steps to follow:
1st – Get permission to bake the cake.
2nd – Gather your supplies.
3rd – Carefully follow the recipe.
4th – Clean up your mess!
5th – Eat your yummy cake!

Mrs. Lincoln's stove was quite different than stoves we use today.

Mary Todd Lincoln's White Cake Recipe

1 cup blanched and chopped ALMONDS

1 cup BUTTER

2 cups SUGAR

3 cups FLOUR

3 teaspoons BAKING POWDER

¼ teaspoon SALT

1 cup MILK

6 EGG WHITES

1 teaspoon VANILLA EXTRACT

CONFECTIONARY SUGAR

Baking Instructions:

Preheat oven to 350 degrees.

Cream butter and sugar.

Add flour and baking powder to creamed butter and sugar, alternating with milk.

Add chopped almonds and mix well.

Beat egg whites until stiff, and fold into the batter.

Stir in vanilla extract.

Pour into greased and floured bundt pan.

Bake 1 hour, or until a toothpick inserted comes out clean.

Cool on a wire rack. When cool, sift confectionary sugar over top.

A basic white frosting sprinkled with almonds was also popular.

My friend decided to try to bake Mary's cake.
It was a messy job!

When Abraham Lincoln became the 16th president of the United States, the Lincolns left their home in Springfield, Illinois, and moved to Washington, D.C., to live in the White House.

The White House when the Lincolns lived there

While living in Washington, D.C., many of Mary's friends from Illinois visited her in the White House. She also made new friends while they lived there.

Friends are important to have. A friend is someone you can talk to and have fun with. My best dog friend is Dakota. She is a corgi. We have lots of fun together.

Dakota and I play together. We are best friends.

One friend Mary made in Washington was a woman named Elizabeth Keckley. Elizabeth was an African-American woman. She had been born a slave. In 1852 she was able to purchase freedom for herself and her son. Elizabeth was a wonderful dressmaker. As the wife of the president, Mrs. Lincoln needed a dressmaker to make sure she always looked her best. Elizabeth became Mary's personal dressmaker. She also became Mrs. Lincoln's closest friend.

A gown Elizabeth made for Mary

Elizabeth Keckley

This picture, taken at the Abraham Lincoln Presidential Museum, shows Mrs. Keckley helping Mrs. Lincoln into one of her beautiful dresses.

Living history interpreters portray
Elizabeth Keckley and Mary Lincoln.

Mrs. Keckley made Mrs. Lincoln many beautiful dresses.
This dress is similar to one she made.

I have to tell you one of my FAVORITE
stories about Mary Lincoln.
Many people have nicknames.
Do you have a nickname?
They are kind of fun to have, I think!
Well, Mr. Lincoln had a wonderful
nickname for Mary.
He called her MOLLY!
I think that is so cool!

The interpreter portraying "Molly" gets a kiss from Molly!

I hope you have enjoyed learning 10 facts about Mary Todd Lincoln.
I think she is an interesting person from history, and I had fun learning about her.

Living history interpreter portraying Mrs. Lincoln

Did you learn any new facts about Mary Todd Lincoln? What is your favorite fact about Mary that you learned? (My favorite is her nickname!) These are the facts I shared:

1. Mary was born December 13, 1818.

2. Mary had many brothers and sisters.

3. Mary learned household skills as a young girl.

4. Games children played.

5. Mary's education.

6. Mary married Abraham Lincoln.

7. The Lincolns had 4 sons.

8. Mary liked to have parties and to bake.

9. Mary had a good friend named Elizabeth Keckley.

10. Mary's nickname was Molly.

One last thing I learned: Mrs. Lincoln never used the name "Mary Todd Lincoln." She always called herself "Mary Lincoln" or "Mrs. Lincoln."
Today we call her Mary Todd Lincoln so we can tell her apart from her daughter-in-law and her granddaughter. They were both Mary Lincolns, too!

Love Molly

Photo Credits:
Opening page: Marla Judge
Molly on a firetruck: Marla Judge
Page 2: Marla Judge
Page 3: Library of Congress (LOC)
Page 6: Marla Judge
Page 9: Marla Judge
Page 10: Both photos: Witnessing History Education Foundation, Inc
Page 11: Marla Judge; Witnessing History Education Foundation, Inc
Page 12: Marla Judge
Page 13: Marla Judge
Page 14: Public Domain
Page 16: LOC; Public Domain x2
Page 17: Marla Judge: LOC
Page 18: Marla Judge
Page 19: All pictures: Marla Judge
Page 20: Both pictures: Marla Judge
Page 21: Marla Judge
Page 22: Public Domain
Page 23: Marla Judge
Page 26: Marla Judge
Page 27: LOC
Page 28: Marla Judge
Page 29: Both pictures: LOC
Page 30: Marla Judge
Page 31: Donna Lounsberry x2
Page 32: Marla Judge
Page 33: Donna Lounsberry
Page 38: Marla Judge

Living History Interpreters:
Pam Brown as Mary Todd Lincoln
www.livingmarylincoln.com
Randy Duncan as Abraham Lincoln
Kathryn Harris as Elizabeth Keckley
William Golladay as Willie Lincoln
Sam Golladay as Tad Lincoln
Katelyn Judge
Abigail Judge
Marla Judge
Beth Staff
Rose Hoehnle
Lillian Shafer
Kehleigha Randall
Fire fighter: Doug Brown

Places to visit:
Lincoln Home National Historic Site
413 S. 8th St. Springfield, Il 62701
Mary Todd Lincoln House
578 W Main St, Lexington, KY 40507
Abraham Presidential Museum and Library
212 N 6th St, Springfield, IL 62701

Movie Resource:
In the Declaration all men are created equal: Abraham Lincoln in Illinois, 1830 to 1860, a film by the Witnessing History Education Foundation, Inc

About the Authors

Molly is a wonderful dalmatian who loves to travel.
At last count she has visited 23 states!
She lives in a big, old house with a huge yard
that she loves to run in (and chase squirrels).
Marla has been married to her husband Robert
for 45 years. They are both retired and enjoy
traveling as much as Molly does.
Before retiring, Marla worked as a school librarian,
a park ranger, and a living history interpreter.
Her love of history and books helps create
this series.

Please write to us at: Mollythehistorydog@gmail.com
Visit: mollythehistorydog.com

Other Books in the Series:

 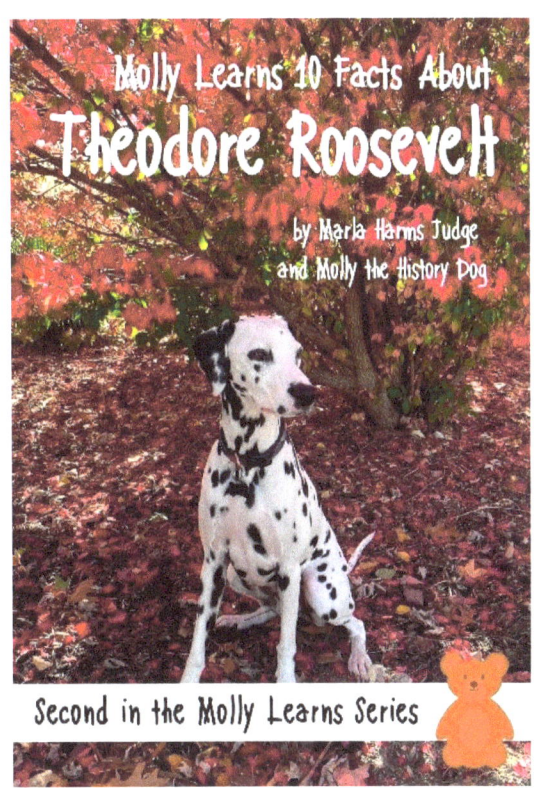

In each book Molly teaches 10 facts about a famous American. She interacts with the readers to keep them involved in the stories!

"This a history lesson children will love. It's fun and interesting, yet written so my novice readers could read it by themselves. I even learned something about Mr. Lincoln I didn't know!"
Reading Specialist Barbara Theilen

How would you decorate Mrs. Lincoln's cake?

www.ingramcontent.com/pod-product-compliance
Lightning Source LLC
Chambersburg PA
CBHW042055050526
44107CB00110B/1188